Helping the Environment

I Can Pick Up Litter

by Mari Schuh

CAPSTONE PRESS
a capstone imprint

For Natalie—MS

Pebble Plus is published by Pebble
1710 Roe Crest Drive, North Mankato, Minnesota 56003
www.mycapstone.com

Library of Congress Cataloging-in-Publication Data
Library of Congress Cataloging-in-Publication Data is available on the Library of Congress website.
ISBN 978-1-9771-0309-3 (library binding)
ISBN 978-1-9771-0519-6 (paperback)
ISBN 978-1-9771-0313-0 (eBook PDF)

Editorial Credits
Anna Butzer, editor; Kayla Rossow, designer;
Tracy Cummins, media researcher; Kathy McColley, production specialist

Image Credits
Alamy: Hill Street Studios/Eric Raptosh, 15; iStockphoto: fstop123, 17, Steve Debenport, 21; Shutterstock: Alfa
Photostudio, 5, Cultura Motion, 13, Dmytro Zinkevych, 11, Kev Gregory, 9, Kumer Oksana, Back Cover, lcswart, 7,
Ms Moloko, Design Element, Pressmaster, 19, R_Tee, Cover

Note to Parents and Teachers

The Helping the Environment set supports national curriculum standards for science and
community. This book describes and illustrates picking up litter. The images support early
readers in understanding the text. The repetition of words and phrases helps early readers
learn new words. This book also introduces early readers to subject-specific vocabulary
words, which are defined in the Glossary section. Early readers may need assistance to read
some words and to use the Table of Contents, Glossary, Read More, Internet Sites, Critical
Thinking Questions, and Index sections of the book.

Printed and bound in China
970

Table of Contents

Lots of Litter

What happened here? Look at all the bottles, cans, and wrappers. Litter is garbage in a place it doesn't belong. I can clean up this litter!

What a Mess!

Litter is dirty and messy. It can spread germs and disease. People and animals can get sick.

Litter floats in rivers and lakes. The water becomes dirty and dangerous. Animals can get tangled up in litter.

Pick Up Litter

I can help get rid of litter. Mom and I pick up litter at a park. We clean up picnic areas, playgrounds, and sports fields too.

We are careful when we pick up litter. We wear thick gloves and bright clothes. Bright colors help others see where we are.

I am careful not to pick up sharp objects. I avoid rusty or heavy items. These things can be unsafe. Dad takes care of these items for me.

I see things that can be recycled. Plastic, glass, and paper go into a recycling bin. Recycling saves energy and resources.

Work Together

I pick up litter, but I also talk
to my friends about litter.
I tell them how important it
is to keep Earth clean.

My friends join me.

Together we pick up litter.

Our community will be a

better place to live!

Glossary

community—a group of people who live in the same area

environment—the natural world of the land, water, and air

litter—garbage that is scattered around carelessly

garbage—anything that is thrown away; other words
for garbage are trash and waste

germ—a very small living thing that causes disease

plastic—a strong, lightweight substance that can be made into
different shapes, such as bottles, containers, and toys

recycle—to make used items into new products; people can
recycle items such as rubber, glass, plastic, and paper

resource—something useful or valuable to a place or person

Read More

Lindeen, Mary. *Reduce, Reuse, Recycle*. A Beginning to Read Book. Chicago: Norwood House Press, 2018.

Miller, Edward. *Recycling Day*. New York: Holiday House, 2015.

Nelson, Robin. *How I Reduce, Reuse, and Recycle*. Responsibility in Action. Minneapolis: Lerner Publications, 2014.

Internet Sites

FactHound offers a safe, fun way to find Internet sites related to this book. All of the sites on FactHound have been researched by our staff.

Here's all you do:

Visit *www.facthound.com*

Type in this code: 9781977103093

Super-cool stuff!

Check out projects, games and lots more at
www.capstonekids.com

Critical Thinking Questions

1. How does litter hurt animals and the environment?

2. Why is it important to pick up litter?

3. What kind of litter can be recycled?

Index